D1466235

Fabulous FASHIONS of the 1920s

Felicia Lowenstein
NIVEN

Fabulous FASHIONS of the DECADES

Enslow Publishers, Inc.
40 Industrial Road
Box 398
Berkeley Heights, NJ 07922
USA

http://www.enslow.com

Library of Congress Cataloging-in-Publication Data

Niven, Felicia Lowenstein.
    Fabulous fashions of the 1920s / Felicia Lowenstein Niven.
        p. cm. — (Fabulous fashions of the decades)
    Fabulous fashions of the nineteen twenties
    Includes bibliographical references and index.
    Summary: "Discusses the fashions of the 1920s, including clothing and hairstyles, trends and fads,
        designers, and world events that influenced the fashion"—Provided by publisher.
    ISBN 978-0-7660-3551-5
    1. Fashion—History—20th century—Juvenile literature. 2. Fashion design—History—20th
        century—Juvenile literature. 3. Lifestyles—History—20th century—Juvenile literature.
        4. Nineteen twenties—Juvenile literature. I. Title. II. Title: Fabulous fashions of the nineteen
        twenties.
    TT504.N56 2011
    746.9'20904—dc22

                                                          2010004194

Paperback ISBN: 978-1-59845-275-4

Printed in the United States of America

052011 Lake Book Manufacturing, Inc., Melrose Park, IL

10 9 8 7 6 5 4 3 2 1

To Our Readers: We have done our best to make sure all Internet Addresses in this book
were active and appropriate when we went to press. However, the author and the publisher
have no control over and assume no liability for the material available on those Internet sites or
on other Web sites they may link to. Any comments or suggestions can be sent by e-mail to comments@
enslow.com or to the address on the back cover.

Illustration Credits: ClassicStock, pp. 20 (woman), 23; Corel Corporation, pp. 5, 20 (gold mask); Courtesy
Everett Collection, p. 18; Dover Publications, Inc./Sears®, pp. 9, 15, 21, 26, 31, 33, 34; The Granger
Collection, NYC – All rights reserved., pp. 1, 8, 17, 24, 25, 27, 29; Keystone/Eyedea/Everett Collection,
p. 14; Library of Congress, pp. 6, 36, 43–45; Louie Armstrong House Museum, p. 40; © Mary Evans Picture
Library/Alamy, p. 4; Mary Evans Picture Library/Everett Collection, p. 10; © 2010 Photos.com, a division
of Getty Images. All rights reserved., p. 47; Rue des Archives/The Granger Collection, NYC – All rights
reserved., pp. 13, 42; Shutterstock, pp. 11, 38.

Cover Illustration: The Granger Collection, NYC – All rights reserved. (flapper chewing gum).

Contents

The 1920s

The 1920s

THE CROSS WORD CRAZE

Crossword puzzles were all the rage in the 1920s. This illustration even shows the dog sporting the look!

Wild and Crazy Fads

You might know someone who is very girly. She probably likes ribbons and flowers and a more romantic style of dress. You also probably know someone who is a tomboy. She prefers a boyish way of dressing.

The 1920s had both. There was a traditional feminine style and a modern boyish one. Women chose the style that suited them best. But feminine and boyish styles in the 1920s were much different from today's fashion.

For example, women—even those who liked the boyish look—did not usually wear pants. If you were a woman wearing pants, it was likely you were going to the beach. The style was called beach pajamas. Otherwise you would not see women dressed that way.

Boyish looks for women meant straight dresses that showed some leg. Feminine designs had billowing skirts, which reached just above the ankle. That was the basic style. But then there was a variety of fads.

Although the women's bathing suits of the 1920s showed off more skin than the ones from the previous decades, they were still fairly conservative. Some beaches even had length requirements. Sometimes, a tape measure was used to make sure a woman's bathing suit was not more than six inches above the knee.

Introduction: Wild and Crazy Fads

Imagine a blouse without sleeves. Then cut off the bottom. You have just created a "chemisette," or mini-blouse. Women in the 1920s tucked chemisettes behind the necklines of their clothes. It looked like they were wearing blouses underneath. That may sound strange to you, but it was very popular at the time. It was also practical. Chemisettes were not as bulky as full blouses.

Women did not wear pants, but boys often wore knee-length pants known as knickers. Men wore "plus fours," which were knickers with an extra four inches of material. When they were fastened at the knee, they ballooned out. This style was more relaxed, and so were the 1920s.

Just look at the bathing suits. Before this time, women wore long skirts to the beach. In the 1920s, bathing suits, and even beach pajamas, showed off figures. Suits had short skirts with shorts underneath and came down to the mid-thigh. It was fashionable to wear heeled shoes with a suit. Now that was a crazy fad!

But maybe the craziest fad of all had to do with stockings. Back then, stockings were made of silk or cotton because nylon had not been invented yet. But the material was not the fad. It was the patterns. These are not patterns you might typically expect on stockings. One popular pattern was the crossword puzzle. But girls with boyfriends would do something even crazier. They would get their boyfriends' faces printed on their stockings! What if they broke up?

Women loved to wear crazy patterned stockings that matched their outfits.

Chapter 1

Hairstyles

Women wore their hair long for centuries. But there was a sense of freedom in the air. World War I had ended. Some women had already cut their hair short, starting back in 1915. More and more women would do so in the 1920s, encouraged by role models in society.

Short hairstyles for women may not seem new to you. But back then, women's salons did not even know how to cut hair short. So women would go to men's barbershops. The cut was called a "bob," probably because it was a word used when cutting a horsetail short. Barbers would "bob" women's long hair in a similar way.

Women wore their hair bobbed in a short blunt cut. Some got a permanent wave to make their hair curly as well as short. Hairstyles ranged from chin-length to very closely cropped to the head. The bob worked well with the fashions of the time, including the hats.

Silent film star Esther Ralston (1902–1994) wore her hair in a wavy bob.

Even women who kept their long hair wore it up. They decorated it with hair ornaments. It seemed that long flowing locks were definitely a thing of the past.

Bring on the Bob

When dancer Irene Castle cut her hair short, it was for convenience. After all, brushing and pinning up long hair took time. Little did she know that women everywhere would be taking note. The "Castle" bob was a blunt cut.

Hairstyles

The hair was cut straight across, just underneath the ears, all around the head. Castle wore it curly with hair brushed off to the side. Women could also wear it with bangs.

Other celebrities followed suit. Silent film actress Clara Bow and Parisian clothes designer Coco Chanel both bobbed their hair. In New York City, there were reports of up to two thousand bobs being cut each day!

Writer F. Scott Fitzgerald even wrote a story about it. "Bernice Bobs Her Hair" revolved around a young lady who was tricked into bobbing her hair, which at the time was a scandalous thing to do. The fictional account appeared in the *Saturday Evening Post*.

The bobby pin was invented to keep bobbed hair looking neat.

Not everybody liked the bob. Some people thought short hair meant the women were risqué, or indecent. As a result, some employers fired workers with bobbed hair.

Some husbands divorced their wives. Preachers spoke about it. Parents complained that they could not tell their daughters from their sons.

Eventually, the controversy died down. This led the way for today's stylish women's haircuts.

Going "Dutch Boy"

The Dutch boy was another kind of bob hairstyle. It was named for the look that Americans associated with a young Dutch boy, as shown on the Dutch Boy brand paint can.

The Dutch boy required very straight hair. The hair was cut straight across just under the ears. Straight bangs completed the look. The hairstyle was worn very flat.

Actress Louise Brooks was famous for her Dutch boy haircut. With her dark locks, it almost looked like she was wearing a helmet.

Show Off a Shingle

The shingle was another kind of bob. It was called a shingle because, in a way, it resembled the shingles on a roof with two separate lengths.

The hair looked like a Dutch boy in the front. But there was an interesting twist—in the back. The hair at the neck was razor cut into a V-shape. The *V* could be seen just below the hairline. Sometimes women added waves or spit curls at the side to dress up this look.

Louise Brooks (1906–1985) and her shiny, black Dutch boy hairstyle graced the cover of *Motion Picture Classic* magazine in October 1926.

Josephine Baker (1906–1975) sported the daring Eton crop, a hairstyle some thought looked very masculine. Baker softened the look by adding spit curls.

Positively Prep: The Eton Crop

African American singer, dancer, and movie star Josephine Baker wore her hair in an Eton crop. This was the shortest hairstyle of the decade. It was considered very daring, perhaps because it showed a woman's ears.

Named after a British boy's prep school, the style was cut very close to the head. At the time, the style looked more male than female. Women would slick their hair back and add a stylish hat to complete the look.

Chapter 2

Women's Styles and Fashion

When you need clothes, you go to the store, right? It was not always that way. Ready-to-wear clothes in stores became available for women at the beginning of the twentieth century. Before that, they went to tailors or dressmakers. Many women sewed their own from cloth and patterns.

Clothes in stores definitely made fashion available to more people and not just wealthy ones. Women liked to follow the fashion trends. In the 1920s, it was fashionable to wear a different outfit for day, afternoon, and evening. Women would change clothes several times a day. The hemline indicated which outfit was for which time of day.

Hemlines, necklines, and waistlines all changed in the 1920s. Necklines and waistlines both dropped down. Hemlines were long in the feminine robe de style, which featured a fitted or straight-cut bodice, a dropped waist, and a full skirt.

There were even new types of undergarments. It was the start of a modern way of dressing.

Boy Oh Boy!

Women were more independent than ever before. They were joining the workforce, and they could vote. Now that they were becoming equal to men, why not dress like them?

The style in the 1920s was "boyish." Women's short hairstyles helped create the look. So did the clothes. Dresses were cut straight, with low waistlines or none at all. The shoulders were broader. The bust was pushed in. Womanly curves disappeared in these new shapeless fashions.

What's Under There?

Underwear also went through a big change. There used to be tight corsets to show a woman's shape. But in the 1920s, it got a little more relaxed. Elastic replaced the stiff bones in corsets. Some women even chose not to wear corsets. Instead they wore camisoles or cami-knickers, which were camisoles with shorts.

Like the dresses of the time, women's suits also hid feminine figures. The boyish look was in style even in the workplace. The woman in blue is even wearing a bow tie!

Evening gowns looked like longer versions of the flapper dress. A black velvet belt cinches the straight-cut dress below the waist.

Other women tried the brassiere (known as the bra today). Brassieres were not exactly new in the 1920s. They had been worn by women since about the start of the twentieth century. But it was not until 1914 that Mary Phelps Jacob patented the first design. It looked like two silk handkerchiefs sewn together. There were ribbons attached for ties.

Like other early brassieres, Jacob's design was meant to flatten rather than shape the bust. Shaped brassieres would not be in style until the next decade.

Flapper Fashion Frenzy

Flappers began appearing around 1917. These were girls who followed a new, wild style. It included galoshes, or rain boots, that they wore unfastened. You could hear them flapping when they walked. That is how they got their name.

One popular flapper fashion was the shift dress. This simple garment was a basic straight dress with a dropped waistline. It was often decorated with fringe. Because its hemline landed just below the knees, the shift dress was ideal for dancing.

Flappers were known for their fashion. They were also known for some bad behavior. They drank alcohol, smoked cigarettes, and applied makeup on in public instead of going to the ladies' room. They even dated men without a chaperone! Until then, proper, well-behaved women did not do any of that. Many people say the flapper opened the door for today's modern woman.

King Tut Mania

Ancient Egyptian pharaoh Tutankhamen's tomb was discovered in 1922. People became fascinated with all things Egyptian. There were clothes and shoes with hieroglyphics. Women wore Cleopatra earrings, snake bracelets, and scarab-shaped jewelry. There were even "mummy" powder compacts.

19

The discovery of King Tutankhamen's tomb resurrected a style that had been dead for thousands of years. Inspired by King Tut's gold funerary mask, women enjoyed looking like ancient royalty.

Chapter 3

Men's Styles and Fashion

For centuries, men had worn the same kind of clothes. Not only was it time to change, but the 1920s also offered the perfect setting. Now that the war was over, people everywhere were ready to become more relaxed.

For one thing, sports clothing became more acceptable as everyday casual wear. The sports clothes back then were more like our dress casual wear today. Men were dressed in trousers and blazers that were made for movement.

Men were seen in single-breasted blazers, sometimes boldly striped. The term *single-breasted* means that there is only one row of buttons down the front and just a narrow overlap of the two sides when they come together.

In contrast, double-breasted jackets have two rows of buttons and a wider overlap. The twenties' blazers were worn with gray flannel or white linen trousers and open-neck shirts. There were the popular, extra-wide Oxford bags and knickerbockers.

That is not to say that men in the 1920s did not wear suits anymore. Some wore the formal styles that had been popular, like the sacque suit. Others tried the new jazz suit and other styles.

Certainly Sacque

Men returning from the war already had a closet filled with clothes. So the beginning of the decade saw its share of the sacque suit. This three-piece suit had been popular since the mid-1800s.

Sacque suits from the 1920s looked a little like three-piece suits worn today. Front pleats on pants were used instead of side ones. Pockets were either slits or openings near the hip. Pants were cuffed. Vests could be made of the same fabric or in contrasting colors and materials.

An Educated Style: Oxford "Bags"

In 1924, students at Oxford University started wearing loose pants with wide legs, as wide as 22 to 40 inches. This gave them a very baggy appearance, hence the name "Oxford bags." Not only that, but some of the pants were

A man dressed in a dashing sacque suit leisurely strolls with an equally fashionable woman.

made in flamboyant colors, such as lavender and pale green! That really made a fashion statement.

The craze soon spread to other college campuses and then to the general public. John Wanamaker, of Wanamaker's Department Store, produced Oxford bags for the American public. They were made of flannel and came in such colors as biscuit (a grayish yellow) and pearl gray.

Knickerbockers were also popular with young men. This ensemble would be typical of an American college student in 1929.

Classically Casual: Knickerbockers

Knickerbockers, or knickers, were considered to be fashionable casual wear for boys. These were loose-fitting trousers that gathered at the knee. They were often worn with kneesocks and sweaters or casual shirts.

Jazz It Up

Unlike the relaxed clothes of the age, the jazz suit was tight-fitting. The jackets were long, and the buttons were placed close together.

Musician Jelly Roll Morton (1890–1941) conducts his band in a snazzy black-and-white jazz suit.

Pants were pencil thin. The suit was associated with jazz lovers and worn by people involved in music and the theatre. Even so, the jazz suit passed in and out of style fairly quickly.

Chapter 4

Accessories

People did not have to be wealthy to be fashionable. Women could take simple dropped-waist dresses and accessorize them.

There was no shortage of accessories in the 1920s. Shawls were a popular way to transform a plain item into something more glamorous. They could be worn at any time of day or night. The shawls also provided additional warmth.

Costume jewelry was also worn by rich and not-so-rich women alike. The jewelry came in colors that could not possibly be natural. It added brightness, sparkle, and shine to the garments it adorned.

Hats were also "all the rage" during this decade. Women wore stylish cloche hats close to their heads. They also sported turbans and other headdresses inspired by the different cultures of Egypt, China, Japan, and Russia.

These two young women show off their individual styles as they enjoy a snack on a ferry in 1928. The girl on the right stands out from the crowd with her boldly printed dress and bare arms, while the girl on the left goes for a more conservative look. They both sport the bell-shaped cloche hats.

Men wore variations of felt hats with a brim, such as the fedora. They also wore top hats for formal occasions and newsboy caps for casual ones.

Women's shoes became a hot new accessory during this time period. Rising hemlines led to a focus on the foot, and women were eager to try new styles. Popular shoes included the bar and T-bar, as well as pumps with tongues, and even harem slippers.

High hemlines also showed off more skin than ever before. Women wore nude stockings on their legs. They might keep their arms bare. It was a big change from what had been in fashion just a decade earlier.

Cloche Call

French hat designer Caroline Reboux created the bell-shaped cloche hat in 1908, although it is mostly associated with the 1920s. It was named after the French word for "bell." The cloche hat was worn pulled down, so it resembled a helmet. The brims were very narrow and eventually disappeared altogether by the late twenties. The cloche hat looked better with short hair, and it inspired many women to cut theirs.

The cloche hat also had its own secret code. Pay attention to the styles with ribbons. If there was a bow, it meant the wearer was single. A knot meant she was married. An untied ribbon showed that the girl had given her promise of love.

American actress Sally Starr (1909–1996) smiles from under her cloche hat in a 1929 photo shoot.

Extra! Extra! Read All About the Newsboy Cap!

If you were a boy or man in the 1920s, you might have worn a newsboy cap. This flat cap looked a little like a beret but had a brim. It was made of tweed or wool. It was a very popular style for men of all ages. But it became associated with newsboys, who often wore it while selling their papers.

Bars and T-bars

New shoe companies sprang up in the 1920s. With shorter hemlines, there was a demand for different styles. People also had money to spend, because the stock market was doing well. There were plenty of factory workers, at home from the war, ready to work, too.

The bar shoe was considered the most classic style of the 1920s. It had a pointed toe, a high heel, and a strap to hold it on the foot while a woman was dancing.

The T-bar shoe, also known as the T-strap, was typical of the era, as well. It was similar to the bar shoe but had another piece of leather that formed a "T" with the strap that attached to the front of the shoe.

Variations of both the bar and the T-bar shoe have been popular in many decades. The always fashionable Mary Jane style of shoe, for example, has a strap that wraps around the ankle. Mary Janes and other types of bar shoes are still made and available today.

For the Woman Who

$4.45
Step-In Pump With Detachable Braided Strap
1SD2814 — Rosewood Satin.
1SD2815 — Black Satin.
Sizes, 2½ to 8. Wide widths only. Be sure to state size. Shipping wt., 1¼ lbs. Beautiful step-in Pump of black or rosewood satin with fancy stitching. Can be worn with or without the braided strap, which is made with elastic going to fit any size foot. New French last, satin covered 2-inch wood heel with Goodyear Wingfoot top lift and extra flexible soles.

The Popular New "Theo" Tie **$3.48**
1SD2778 — Tan Leather.
1SD2779 — Patent Leather.
Sizes, 2½ to 8. Wide widths only. Be sure to state size. Shipping wt., 1¼ lbs.
The one-eyelet "Theo" Tie is one of the newest things out. Comes in tan or black patent leather. Is made over the new French last. Has a military heel, 1¾ inches high, with a rubber top lift. The cut-outs add to its coolness and neatness.

$4.95 Superb in Style!
1SD2830 Sizes, 2½ to 8. Wide widths only. Be sure to state size. Shipping wt., 1¼ lbs.
Superb in style, design and quality is this dainty step-in Pump of tan calfskin with field mouse color leather back. A very attractive combination that is unusually appealing to women of exquisite taste. Built over the new French last, which is the most popular in women's footwear. Has the field mouse color leather covered wood military heel, 1¾ inches high, with the Goodyear Wingfoot rubber top lift. A small ornament in the front adds to its attractiveness.

A Blond Satin That Is Up to the Minute in Style **$4.75**
1SD2831 — Sizes, 2½ to 8. Wide widths only. Be sure to state size. Shipping wt., 1 lb.
The new light shades of satin footwear are necessary to complete any well dressed woman's wardrobe. Here's a one-strap model of blond satin with fancy stitching that will fill that need. Built on the new French last. Has blond satin covered wood military heel, 1¾ in. high, with Goodyear Wingfoot top lift.

All Shoes on This Page Have Light Color Linings That Prevent the Soiling of the Most Delicate Shades of Hosiery.

Practical as Well as Up to Date and Dressy
$2.98 1SD2825 Sizes, 2½ to 8. Wide widths only. Be sure to state size. Shipping wt., 1¼ lbs.
Another one-eyelet "Theo" Tie that is very practical as well as up to date and dressy. Is made of patent leather on a medium round toe last. Has a low walking heel, 1 inch high, with rubber top lift. A sensible but attractive model. Sure to please.
Patent Leather

Stylishly Smart **$2.98**
1SD2767 — Tan Leather.
1SD2768 — Patent Leather With Tan.
Sizes, 2½ to 8. Wide widths only. Be sure to state size. Shipping wt., 1¼ lbs.
One of the smarter fall styles for the well dressed woman. The ribbon tie and the cut-out in tan or patent leather give it a graceful model.

Newest in Ties **$3.98**
1SD2736 — Sizes, 2½ to 8. Wide widths only. Be sure to state size. Shipping wt., 1¼ lbs.
Something real new in Ties that is sure to be very popular. Made of patent leather with tan leather underlay. Is built on a medium round toe last and has a low heel, 1 inch high, with a rubber top lift.

Well Dressed Woman's Choice **$3.95**
1SD2696 — Sizes, 2½ to 8. Wide widths only. Be sure to state size. Shipping wt., 1¼ lbs.
The well dressed woman's choice this season is the two-eyelet ribbon Tie. This new style feature looks exceptionally well on the black satin, black suede trimmed model shown here. Made over the new French last and has light color linings. Satin covered 1¾-inch wood heel with Goodyear Wingfoot top lift.

1SD2783 — Sizes, 2½ to 8. Wide widths only. Be sure to state size. Shipping wt., 1¼ lbs. **$3.98**
One of the newest styles direct from the world's great style centers. Everybody is raving about this one-strap model. It is made in black patent leather vamp and rust kid leather back. This makes a pretty, attractive model.
Patent Leather

236

World's Largest Store

This Sears® catalog page features some of the different designs bar shoes came in. The straps could have bows, braids, or fancy buttons to give them more flair.

Dare to Bare It

Up until the 1920s, women's clothes had covered most of their bodies. Fashions went from their necks to their knuckles and down past their ankles. The previous decade had hemlines that showed women's shoes for the first time. But the 1920s really went far past that.

Women in the 1920s appeared more "naked" than ever before. Evening gowns showed off long slender arms. Shorter day dresses showed legs.

Beige-colored stockings created a "bare" look. Made of silk or artificial silk known as rayon, the stockings were often so shiny that girls used powder to dull them. The stockings were affordable, so anyone could enjoy this fashionable look.

Chapter 5

Fads and Trends

In the 1920s, there was plenty of experimentation with fashion. This led to some short-lived fads and to some trends that are still with us today.

Some trends, like the zipper, were accessible to everyone. After all, one did not have to be wealthy to buy clothes with the new zippers. Other fads, like raccoon coats, were enjoyed only by people with money.

"Step-in" Undergarments

If you traveled back in time before the 1920s, you would not recognize your underwear. Women and girls wore stiff bone corsets that laced up tightly to cinch in their waists. A woman could not even dress herself; she needed help lacing the corset.

FINE QUALITY

De Luxe SILK UNDERWEAR

We ask that our customers give special attention to the high grade silk crepe de chine, messalines, satins and laces used on all our silk underwear. These, combined with excellent workmanship, make our silk line one which will offer service and satisfaction. We are showing conservative but latest styles, which will charm the wearer of silk underwear.

Price, Each $3.48
38E9740—Flesh. Women's Fine Quality Silk Crepe de Chine Envelope Chemise. Front and back trimmed with insertions of good quality lace and silk satin. Top and bottom neatly edged with lace. Attractively finished in front with two rows of shirring. Has silk ribbon draw and rosettes. Sizes, 34 to 44 inches bust measure. State size. Shipping weight, 12 ounces.

Price, $2.48 Each
38E9776—White. Women's Vestee. Body made of good quality crepe de chine, Front made with plaited ruffles of high grade net and finished at top with row of hemstitching. Ribbon and shoulder straps and draw. Elastic at waist. A very popular garment which may be worn in place of a waist with a suit or sweater. Sizes, 34 to 44 inches bust measure. State size. Shipping weight, 10 oz.

Price, $1.38 Each
38E4598—Flesh. Women's Silk Satin Bandeau. Trimmed in front with neat pattern good quality lace and edged at top with lace to match. Ribbon shoulder straps and draw string. Elastic in back. Closes in back with hooks and eyes. Sizes, 32 to 48 inches bust measure. State size. Shipping wt., 10 oz.

Price, $1.49 Each
38E4599—Flesh. Women's Bandeau. Made of good quality washable satin. Front and sides neatly shirred. Top and front trimmed with lace edging. Has rosette and ribbon shoulder straps. Rustproof boning. Elastic in back. Closes in back with hooks and eyes. A very attractive bandeau. Sizes, 32 to 48 inches bust measure. State size. Shipping weight, 10 ounces.

Price, $2.98 Each
38E9766—Flesh. Women's High Grade Crepe de Chine Bloomers. Bottoms neatly finished with hemstitching and ribbon bows. Reinforced at waist and crotch which insures extra wear. Elastic at waist and knees. Sizes, small, medium and large. State size. Shipping weight, 14 ounces.

Price, $3.58 Each
38E9713—Flesh. Women's High Grade Washable Satin Bloomers. Neatly finished at bottoms with elastic and hemstitched ruffles. Have elastic at waist and knees. Reinforced at crotch. Sizes, small, medium and large. State size. Shipping weight, 1⅛ pounds.

Price, $3.98 Each
38E9743—Flesh. Women's Fine Quality Silk Crepe de Chine Combination. Front and back attractively finished with shirred white satin ribbon. Closes at side. Double shoulder straps of same material. Ribbon draw. Front have rosettes. Bottoms have elastic at knees and ruffles edged with satin ribbon and trimmed with rosettes. Crotch closes with snap fasteners. Sizes, 34 to 44 inches bust measure. State size. Shipping weight, 14 ounces.

Price, $3.98 Each
38E9708—Brown and shamrock changeable.
38E9709—Purple.
38E9710—Navy blue.
38E9711—Flesh.
Women's High Grade Silk Messaline Bloomers. Reinforced at crotch. Elastic at waist and at knees. Finished at bottoms with small ruffles. Length, 27 inches. Shipping weight, 1 pound.

Price, $4.98 Each
38E9755—Flesh.
38E9756—Black.
38E9757—Navy blue.
38E9758—Copenhagen blue.
38E9759—Blue and green changeable.
38E9760—Plum.
Women's High Grade Three-Quarter Length Messaline Silk Bloomers. Neatly finished at bottom with two rows of elastic. Elastic waistband. Reinforced crotch. Length, 33 inches. Shipping weight, 1 pound.

The 1920s saw the freedom of step-in underwear. Women, and men, stepped into all-in-one undergarments. Separates were also available.

A Dress in an Hour?

It was faster and easier for women to get dressed in the 1920s than ever before. That led the way for the "one hour dress." Introduced by the Women's Fashion Institute, this dress could be sewn at home in just about an hour.

The dress was advertised as the perfect choice when a woman was invited last minute to a party and she had nothing to wear. When it first came out, it was demonstrated in Grand Central Palace, New York. The dress was made there in thirty-four minutes.

This catalog page shows all the different types of undergarments for women. At the top left is a chemise, which is a style of sleepwear still worn today. The woman standing up at the bottom left wears an all-in-one, or combination, garment, which closes at the side. The separates include a top called a vestee, decorated with fringe in the front, which women could wear underneath a blazer or sweater; bandeaus, or brassieres in the shape of a band that go across the bust; and bloomers, which were roomy, billowy bottoms.

Mary La Follette, a socialite, in her warm and cozy full-length raccoon coat, is ready for a night on the town!

Reserve a Raccoon

If you were a college student in the 1920s, you might own a raccoon coat. These gray-and-black coats were fashionable because they were flashy. Raccoon, one of the cheaper furs, was affordable to students—well, at least the wealthier ones. They were also popular with the people who owned cars. Back in those days, automobiles were wide open, and the fur coats kept the passengers warm.

Zip It Up!

Around 1920, zippers started appearing on clothes. They were not used widely, though. After all, zippers are metal. They rusted whenever the clothes were washed.

American manufacturer B. F. Goodrich rustproofed the zippers and used them on a new line of rubber boots. He named them Zipper Boots, and they were a huge hit.

Designers began to experiment with zippers. It would not be long before they would be on clothes. They began to be used on men's trousers and children's clothes in the 1920s. By the 1930s, designer Elsa Schiaparelli would use them on her high-fashion designs.

Chapter 6
Pop Culture

At first glance, it seemed the 1920s was a happy time. World War I had ended, and the soldiers were home. People were spending money. There was plenty of entertainment. There were movies with sound, radio broadcasts, jazz music, dancing, and more.

But it was not all it appeared to be. There was a growing gap between rich and poor. The wealthy were spending only a small part of their incomes as compared to everyone else. There was also a lot of unemployment.

In fact, the average person did not have the money to buy all that he or she wanted. So the concept of credit was introduced. Buying now and paying later was very popular. It was also the beginning of an unstable economy.

The Eighteenth Amendment to the Constitution also took effect in the 1920s. Known as "Prohibition," the law meant that people were no longer allowed to drink alcohol. The lawmakers thought it would help family life.

Some people drank anyway in secret. Prohibition was unpopular, and it was not always enforced. Eventually, the government realized that it was not working. It repealed the Eighteenth Amendment in 1933.

Radio and All That Jazz

The first commercial radio broadcast took place on November 2, 1920. Station KDKA out of Pittsburgh, Pennsylvania, broadcast the results of the Harding–Cox presidential race. Over the next four years, there would be as many as six hundred commercial stations around the country. People started to hear the same music, and news traveled faster than ever.

One type of music that probably would not have been heard on those early radio broadcasts was jazz. The freestyle arrangements of jazz music were seen as somewhat naughty. The jazz movement started in New Orleans among the African-American population. As they left the town to seek work, the music went with them. By the 1920s, jazz was heard not just in the South but also in Harlem, New York.

Noted jazz musicians included Louis Armstrong, Joe "King" Oliver, and Edward "Kid" Ory. Jazz music was enjoyed in nightclubs and dance halls. It was so popular during this time that the 1920s was called "the Jazz Age."

Jazz legend Louis Armstrong (1901–1971) sits at the piano with other musicians. He is famous for his trumpet playing and scatting, or singing improvised nonsensical syllables to music.

The Charleston Craze

Step back with your right foot. Kick back with your left. You have just done the first steps of the Charleston, a popular dance craze in the 1920s.

The dance has been traced back to African Americans. It was named for the area where it was probably invented, an island off Charleston, South Carolina.

The dance was perfect for music with a fast beat. Flappers loved to do it. The fringes and beads would swing wildly. The Charleston could be danced alone, with a partner, or in a group.

Talking Movies

"Wait a minute. You ain't heard nothin' yet!" Those were the first words spoken in a movie. The year was 1927, the actor was Al Jolson, and the movie was *The Jazz Singer*. It was the first talking motion picture. Up until then, people watched silent movies with a pianist playing at the movie house. The tempo of the music would change depending on what was happening on-screen.

With talking films, there was no longer a need for subtitles or exaggerated motions. Hollywood started producing many types of movies, such as westerns, epics, dramas, and romance. In fact, many more movies were made in the 1920s than are made today.

These women are dancing the night away in a Charleston dance contest in New York. How long can you dance without stopping?

Staying Power

There were many tests of staying power in the 1920s. The dance marathons had dancers going nonstop for days, competing for prize money. They had to dance for forty-five minutes out of each hour around the clock. In many cases, people slept while being held up by their partners.

Timeline

The 1920s

The look: cloche hats, dropped-waist dresses, long strands of pearls (women), and baggy pants (men)

The hair: short bobs

The fad: raccoon coats

The 1930s

The look: dropped hemlines, natural waists, practical shoes (women), and blazers and trousers (men)

The hair: finger waves and permanents

The fad: sunbathing

The 1940s

The look: shirtwaist dresses and military style (women) and suits and fedoras (men)

The hair: victory rolls and updos

The fad: kangaroo cloaks

The 1950s

The look: circular skirts and saddle shoes (women) and the greaser look (men)

The hair: bouffants and pompadours

The fad: coonskin caps

The 1960s

The look: bell-bottoms and miniskirts (women) and turtlenecks and hipster pants (men)

The hair: beehives and pageboys

The fad: go-go boots

The 1970s

The look: designer jeans (women) and leisure suits (men)

The hair: shags and Afros

The fad: hot pants

(The) 1980s

The look: preppy (women and men) and *Miami Vice* (men)

The hair: side ponytails and mullets

The fad: ripped off-the-shoulder sweatshirts

(The) 1990s

The look: low-rise, straight-leg jeans (both women and men)

The hair: the "Rachel" cut from *Friends*

The fad: ripped, acid-washed jeans

(The) 2000s

The look: leggings and long tunic tops (women) and the sophisticated urban look (men)

The hair: feminine, face-framing cuts (with straight hair dominating over curly)

The fad: organic and bamboo clothing

Glossary

accessible—Easily available to everyone.

billowing—Flaring out or bulging.

blunt (cut)—Cutting the hair straight across so that lengths of hair form one level.

bodice—The part of the dress from the shoulder to the waist.

conservative—Traditional in style.

controversy—A debate where there is strong disagreement on both sides.

corset—A close-fitting undergarment worn to support and to shape a woman's body.

double-breasted—A jacket style where one side of the garment overlaps the front of the other side; double-breasted jackets usually have a double row of buttons.

flamboyant—Bright and colorful, easily noticed.

flapper—A rebellious young woman of the 1920s.

hieroglyphics—A picture writing system used in ancient Egypt.

leisurely—In a relaxed way.

pump—A slip-on woman's shoe with a medium or high heel.

scarab—A type of beetle that was considered godlike by the ancient Egyptians.

single-breasted—A style of jacket with a single row of buttons and just a narrow overlap of the two sides when they come together.

trend—The current style or general direction of fashion.

trousers—An old-fashioned word for men's pants.

undergarments—Garments worn next to the skin and under clothes.

Further Reading

Books

Beker, Jeanne. *Passion for Fashion: Careers in Style*. Toronto, Canada: Tundra Books, 2008.

Herald, Jacqueline. *Fashions of a Decade: The 1920s*. New York: Facts on File, 2006.

McEvoy, Anne. *The 1920s and 1930s*. New York: Bailey Pub. Associated, 2009.

McKissack, Lisa Beringer. *Women of the Harlem Renaissance*. Minneapolis, Minn.: Compass Point Books, 2007.

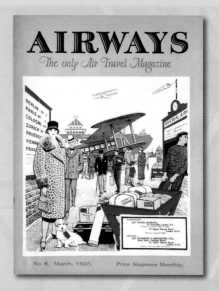

Internet Addresses

Fashion-Era, "Flapper Fashion 1920s"
<http://www.fashion-era.com/flapper_fashion_1920s.htm>

1920-30.com, "Women's Fashions 1920s"
<http://www.1920-30.com/fashion/>

Index